OR
CURRENT
RESIDENT

Also by Thomas Fink

Poetry

Surprise Visit (Domestic Press, 1993)
Gossip (Marsh Hawk Press, 2001)
After Taxes (Marsh Hawk Press, 2004)
No Appointment Necessary (Moria Poetry, 2006)
Clarity and Other Poems (Marsh Hawk Press, 2008)
Autopsy Turvy [with Maya D. Mason] (Meritage Press, 2010)
Peace Conference (Marsh Hawk Press, 2011)
Joyride (Marsh Hawk Press, 2013)
Selected Poems & Poetic Series (Marsh Hawk Press, 2016)
Hedge Fund Certainty (Meritage Press and I.E. Press, 2019)
A Pageant for Every Addiction [with Maya D. Mason] (Marsh Hawk Press, 2020)
Zeugma (Marsh Hawk Press, 2022)

Chapbooks

Staccato Landmark (Beard of Bees, 2006)
Generic Whistle Stop (Portable Press at YoYo Labs, 2009)
Yinglish Strophes (Truck Books, 2009)
Former Sestinas [with Tom Beckett] (Beard of Bees, 2013)

Criticism and Pedagogy

The Poetry of David Shapiro (Fairleigh Dickinson University Press, 1993)
"A Different Sense of Power": Problems of Community in Late-Twentieth Century U.S. Poetry (Fairleigh Dickinson University Press, 2001)
Reading Poetry with College and University Students: Overcoming Barriers and Deepening Engagement (Bloomsbury Academic, 2022)

Co-Edited Books

With Tuzyline Jita Allan. *Literature Around the Globe* (Kendall/Hunt, 1995)
With Joseph Lease. *"Burning Interiors": David Shapiro's Poetry and Poetics* (Fairleigh Dickinson University Press, 2007)
With Judith Halden-Sullivan. *Reading the Difficulties: Dialogues with Contemporary American Innovative Poetry* (University of Alabama Press, 2014)

OR CURRENT RESIDENT

poems

Thomas Fink

Marsh Hawk Press
East Rockaway, New York·2025

7 6 5 4 3 2 1 FIRST EDITION

Marsh Hawk Press books are published by Poetry Mailing List, Inc., a not-for-profit corporation under section 501 (c) 3 United States Internal Revenue Code.

Cover Painting: Thomas Fink, "All the Livelong Night." Acrylic on canvas, 2024.
Painting of Author: Detail in untitled painting by Maya Mason, oil on canvas, 2023.

Book Design: Susan Quasha
Titles set in Futura and text in Adobe Garamond Pro

Library of Congress Cataloging-in-Publication Data

Names: Fink, Thomas, 1954- author.
Title: Or current resident / Thomas Fink.
Description: First edition. | East Rockaway, New York : Marsh Hawk Press, 2025.
Identifiers: LCCN 2024055021 | ISBN 9798990249004 (paperback)
Subjects: LCGFT: Poetry.
Classification: LCC PS3606.I55 O7 2025 | DDC 811/.6—dc23/eng/20241121
LC record available at https://lccn.loc.gov/2024055021

16 17 18 19 20   7 6 5 4 3 2 1   FIRST EDITION

MHP
Marsh Hawk Press
P.O. Box 206, East Rockaway, N.Y. 11518-0206
mheditor@marshhawkpress.org

For all my students who have been committed to their intellectual and aesthetic growth

Contents

OR
CURRENT
RESIDENT

MISSION STATEMENT 1

Never a nanosecond   squandered on
ex-knowledge   elegies. To dash
into the shortest   queue for
exquisite tech   pivots. With

dry ice   severity, to

ratiocinate so   an elliptical
defense blinds   each approaching
worm. Essence distillation: a given.
Enduring requires surplus essence.

MISSION STATEMENT 2

We invest in oracle-proof tactics & relegate incompetent
umbrellas to alley cans.   Dimpled monopolies cannot
cow us. As the slumming   elite engage in imperial
caterwauling while   pow(d)ering their wi(n)gs,

we unmask &   upend pseudonymous raids

that groom   hyperbolic unrest through a

new nationalism   conceived in libido.
No pushers of   secular psalm oil,
we submit that,   to halt ecstatic poison
flow, abrasive   medicine   must be prescribed.

MISSION STATEMENT 3

Our aim: to make competence immortal so that traditionally
bumpy interface between   technical infrastructure &
peevish, addled end-users   grows smooth as solid-state

telepathy. To this end, noble   as it is self-perpetuating,

we are laboring to assemble the   most eminent team
of math educators, cognitive   psychoengineers,
& simplicity gurus accessible to corporate civilization.

MISSION STATEMENT 4

We'll descend on any ungated spiritual neighborhood.
The prime objective is harvesting irrational
affections in our cherished team & clientele alike.
For the former, business leisure. (In mod
eration.) For the latter, an explosive

variety of sheens served with gobbets of honest

home-cooked goodness. A few more windows
will make it cohere. Further, aromatherapeutic
instinct has yet to fail us. All this so that even
when a defective egg is laid, our abiding good
will & earnest helpfulness stand, indisputable.

MISSION STATEMENT 5

To capture longevity, our cherished yardstick in
volves what is not   to be excused:
executives puking   crescendo,

groin grammar ex   position, sugar fog

cultivation, exploitation of vanity, paragon
impersonator music—   the usual road
to rapid earnings. & next, disintegration.

MISSION STATEMENT 6

Paying too little mind to data truancy— that was
our ghastly error, along with trusting the power
of a majority, given plain facts, to thrust aside
brands of imitation morality & opt for urgent

detergent. No more! Never will we

stint on fealty to home audience criteria,

however corn-drenched the elites may….
The mission we now shoulder: easing
fledgling liberators into congruence
with varnished imperative soundings.

CEO COLLIDES WITH BRUTE PARADOX

We press hard-working myths full
of quoted passion into the service
of capital
accumulation.
Much actualized
delusion is rich
soil
for the
luminous fewest. Yet abject
valleys' fantasy
consumption oft
triggers shadowy
slowdowns, clerical
fuckups, mental truancy—
stepping on efficient
redistribution from
crass labor
all the way
to the
golden
apex.

BUMPY SINGALONG

Minstrels in uniformed
bondage.
Trumpet groaning:
Systemic
Disney
abuse.
Frisbees

flood an underground garage. Unmute the music
energy device:
Streets

are dancing
in the children.

COLD CALLING

This morning's solitude

was delicious.
Now expired. Two muscular

ghosts, however, see to it that no mortal
separates me from my
inherited bounty.

Hello,
who are you? Don't lay
that "no one understands" on us. Learn
to draw already.

Well,
perhaps you lack
directions? We will
provide. Wherever you long
to travel.

"YOU GET WHAT YOU PAY FOR"

Last August I
was behind on my
future.   Proactivity: more
than urgent. I
bought that
spouse (beside the blinds). The sales advocate

was devoid   of caveat
empathy,   but then my
motives tend to   narrow. Operating
instructions injected
a disfiguring

haplessness. You wouldn't believe what
didn't happen. (A minimum expected.)
Would a robot

act more
cost-efficient? Those in my

range exude metal— fully exposed.

A BRIEF SURVEY

Since you recently frequented Upland Stony Brothel, your
feint would be feverishly
cherished. Our gold is to provide the best poseurs'
mediocre caress carols
& feminist goblet offerings to our patriot patriarchs
& to mold vixen vocabulary
to be melodramatically marketable

as perversion permits.
Kindly take a few miscellaneous misconstructions
to submit what you think of the
caricature you requited. It is
more than impotent for us to

knead every honest oracle extemporizing
on misdeeds tethered to
vodka vitamins.
Your commiserations will be reviewed soulfully by

adulterers, pickaxes, &
nutcrackers & will enable us to inch toward
incandescence: liberation of carnivorous cargo

that we denude. "Oh, mirror, your work
dissatisfies me. Go melt

in shame."

DREAM JOB POSTINGS

Epithet chancellor for
a scrounging
comics' guild.

Icon physician for
a third tier
advertising joint.

Epigram engineer for
an as yet
underbooked
motivational
speakers' stable.

Windbag condenser
for well-endowed
political newbies.

A once
pristine precinct's
graffiti undertaker.

Subculture
tabernacle
receptionist.

UFO documentarian
for a profitable
new TV series.

Ghost-association
liaison with
abject skeptics.

Dream obfuscator
for the perennially
terrified.

Virtual bodyguard
for the CEO of
an AI startup.

The Displaced
Thespians Bureau's
grimace counselor.

Labyrinth tactician
for a clandestine
council of sincere
war mongers.

Contingency
concierge for
the Jasmine
Nuclear Compound.

Marital translator for
a clinic serving
chronically
perplexed couples.

The Coalition for
the Socially
Hapless's Junior
Snafu Editor.

Absolution clerk
for the congregation
of Our Lady of
Perpetual Latitude's
Special Contributions
Subcommittee.

Honor restoration
associate for
the Dimmed
Stars Talent
Agency.

Assistant Beard
Pimp for
Invisibility Plus.

Alibi facilitator
for Defense
at Any Cost.

Permissive
chaperone for
the Warren G.
Harding Middle
School Prom.

The Northwest
Prairie Zoo
Without Cages'
Chief Lion
Companion.

Absence framer
for the Metaphysics
Division of
Cutting Edge
Petrol Unlimited.

Vacuum historian
for the Hegemony
Maintenance
Consortium.

Reassurance
agent for the
Society for
Annihilation
of Human
Reticence.
The Second &
Third Chance

Network's
indigenous
dignity publicist.

Consciousness
lifeguard for
Supreme
Eco Park.

Afterlife projectionist
for the Scientific
Psychics Alliance.

Status leveler
for the Marxist
Elite Collective.

Middle-class
gourmet fundraiser.

Misfortune teller
for Humble Pie
Hospital for
the Smug.

South Precipice
Elementary
School's
motivational
fuckup.

Lethal toastmaster
for the Jaded
Correspondents'
Association
Monthly Banquet.

The Wall
Street on Steroids
Middle Management
Training Program's
Harassment motivator.

Financial deckhand
for Speculative
Flood Ltd.

Reverse psych
influencer
at the Center
for Narcissist
Remodeling.

Ratio engineer
for Home Product
Value Inflation Service

Lavish Pollution
Cartel's Inconvenient-
data deflater.

Chemistry crew
member for Placebo
Manufacturing
Syndicate.

Material resources
coordinator for
Quicksand
Paving
Corporation.

Cistern beautifier
for Camouflage
Realty Firm.

Outhouse-rejuvenation
subsubsubcontractor
for Consolidated
Farms of Tick-
borne County.

Public rest
room & truck
stop critic for
Pristine Magazine.

Executive body
double for
a leading
multinational
arms dealer.

Psychotic
billionaire's
codependent.

Claim dissolver
for the loop
hole factory
of Aporia
Mutual
Insurance Co.

Industrial
extortionist
for a thriving
dark web
enterprise.

System Galore's
Obsolescence
planner.

Refund redeemer
for Disgruntled 'R Us.

Chief Exemption
procurer for
Ambidextrous
Accounting.

Federal-Contract-
Payola League's
host & prime
facilitator.

Surplus concealer
for the Gentle
Taxation Council.

Uncharitable
mistrust
counsel for
Philanthro
pists Requited.

American
Dream
House's
Budget gap
plugger.

Celebrity
Impersonator
for a chain
of speakeasys

Vice President
of Mimetic
Acquisitions
for an AI
Cartel.

Caprice officer
For Beyond
Bounds Studio.

Orgy MC
at Studio 24.

Ecclesiastical
pornographer
for an inter
denominational
sanctuary's ad
department.

Laugh-track
chorus conductor
for Tragi
comedy Plus.

Domestic
Criminal
Circle's
invisible
shoplifter.

Repute
eviscerator
for a sink
ing hopeful.

Pseudo kidnap
victim for
a promising
extortion house.

Human decoy
for a series of
international
stings.

Designated writher
for a Pathos
Enrichment Club.

The Deadbeat
Advisory Board's
neglect perfumer.

Angst enhancement
officer for the Army
Corps of Nuclear
Innovators.

Regime stabilizer
for Will T.
Power Consultants.

Terrorist recruiter
for None of Their
Business & Associates.

Social entropy
director for
Random Plot
Productions.

Fracas organizer
for Citizens
against Stifling
Tranquility.

Volcano tamer
for the Impossible
Dream Engine
Partnership.

Toxic waste site
janitor for Global
Impasse Corporation.

The Racist Sexist
Homophobic
Community Center's
spiritual arsonist.

Tyrant poisoner
for the Moral
Efficiency Institute.

Riot consultant
for Satanic
Schadenfreude
Unbounded.

Schism
facilitator
for Political
Psychopaths
Bargain Base.

Bazooka
sanctifier
for the Holy
War Con
sortium.

Lawyers
in Defense
of the Seem
ingly Inde
fensible's
election
returns
denial
promoter.

Grassroots-
momentum
destabilizer
for Oligarchs
Unbridled.

Cheerful
scapegoat
for Intractable
Dilemma Man
agers, Inc.

An untraceable
PAC's soapbox
architect.

Injustice molester
for the Quasi-Utopian
Theatre Troupe.

Dirty secret
extractor for the
International Enquirer.

Junta navigator
for Gold & Gold
Speculative Instruments.

The U.N. Security
Council's Vice-Epicenter
Chamberlain.

Intergalactic
communications
specialist for
Untrammeled Solutions.

Pun therapist for People
for the De-reification
of Humorless Curmudgeons.

Licensed shapeshifter
for Identity Construction
without Borders.

GENTLE REMINDER:

Next Friday

is a Monday
schedule. No unilateral

home
office whim,
it issues from

a singular priority initiative grindstone
group's deliberation. On "Friday,"
you'll onboard
a cascade

of freshly picked
influencers decked
in enviable unemployment
records. (We'll
cull

a few
for rhyme management
training.) Should you
pop into
the office that day
with a Friday

attitude, foreshadow a crisp vocal
slap. Yet if you
cotton
to this imperative, the nonsense
within your accuracy
will greet the accuracy
inside our nonsense.

REMAIN SEATED.

Do not   stack

legacies on top of one another.
Return   the father
to its original   position. Administer

a vapid heartbeat. Breathe nominally. If lungs demand more
spirit,   hack
into a nearby   eternity.
A life vent   may be
underneath. Remain seated, greeting

emergency impact.   Photography is
forbidden   during
visible   crisis.

Await destruction(s).

BUREAU

Whispering scissors.

Bureaucracy vows
to sparkle.

To expound the mundane ecstatic. Beyond
a wooden mood. For all
present, if not all

accounted for. (Bookmark any stray charisma.) Gregarious
wisteria rises
from asphalt
road faults.

AFFRONT TO CENTER AND CIRCUMFERENCE

Muster courage for precautions.

Duck obvious
arrows. Maintain

a prudent distance
from lifeboat thrashers
& sheepskin boomerangs. Your safety remains pertinent

to us: litigation
bashes a budget already teetering.
When some nudnik messes with the top
layer of the palimpsest, contagion

will burgeon. Listen: half this
Congress is unhinged. Lawfuckers with backwater
growls, tethered to praxis

bold as lava, steer a revolution
to seed virtual

autocracy.

TREND SPIN

Welkin

waxes raging chemical blue. Last
month on

Cable, where common
graphic narrative armature gets dosed
with hyperbole, central eccentricities were naturalized.

This strikes at
some unprotected
core: eccentric demographics' nod
to a banal familiar. (No elitist

laugh track infiltration
could
dam[n] it.)

Normality, bemused,
lobbies for its next

spin.

HIDDEN IN PLAIN SITE

Credit publicists
for keeping the cognitively
thin inflated.
Until lately, fiscal acrobats
could shield him from transparency.

Still, lethal weeds bloom from asphalt. Narcissistic
statutes continue to ignite moronic
fatalities.
Fart concertos

across the plains fog this. A resumé
of his misadventures
is inadmissible

to those whose newsfeeds provide
journalistic massacre
of the opposition.

LOSS

Isn't it rare to pin down a core
demographic merely through

public riffing? Intuitively to honor traffic
laws
of asexual seduction, to layer

disruptive insinuations, leap
over audience will to thought.
Cherished
public furniture was soon t(h)rashed.

PTSD has taken
wing across 4 time
zones. We're leering
at a hole in a mirror. This
loser

cannot
conceive
of any angle from which he could
have lost
or would ever lose.
Unless in the privacy of the unconscious.

THE CAFÉ DRUGS

its prisoners
efficiently. Sunshine writhes at the slum

beach.
Terrorist homily
tattoos a horizon.

Post-mortem condemnation
of bleached
pigs, slimy
llamas. Evangelical tumult. "Welcome,

trespassers!"
Termites home
cozily in the pulpit. Greeting a monsoon,
their god, spent,
repents.

DOGGED

dogma. Prophecy
predictable.
Grinning furnace.
"Death

is the

audience."
Penance permanent.
This
thinking thins.

VEXATION ZONE

Snakes rise
through triangles. Veins salute.
No solid
lid
on id.
Satin rats
tacitly ratify
riot rite,
fragment
judgment.

MEMORY TACTICS

A fistful
of mustard. Gulped whole.
The fact spawning the occasion

is often repeatedly force fed.

He feigns ill.

To bypass depression-
inducing gatherings. A sealed lid
can be trusted. Let fine memories prevail.

SARTORIAL IDEOLOGIES '68 (SONNINA)

The father prays his son will conform
to '68 Madison Avenue shop attire, will learn
groomed business class virtues, even if to conform
means to learn
to live beyond means. Fear of the hippy dippy dress
code

infects the father's stream. But to dress
according to any code
is to forget how sartorial
ideology frays in time. The son shops haphazardly, without
thought of sartorial
coordination & consistency. Without

environmental momentum, the father
waits in his suit for the son to turn into a father.

HASTY OBIT

Grey

web of
gloom. Untimely.

See
how we're
vibrating? 4

hours
hence—retracted.
First, solace.
Next,
fury over

gratuitous compassion.
"Unknown"
with same

name? Or
death

wish shared?

YINGLISH STROPHES 31

They don't recognize you

the minute they get
elected. Before—they're all
over you. Marriage optimum

a beautifully soul to
with. My cousins for
youngest bashful always on
the outlook. Is brisket
shopping this? Retrospect that

forty, fifty—a glimpse
may have then to
quality a soul. Finds
the take with the
give. Trying to equal.
Attentive some days enough
being marital. Or political.

YINGLISH STROPHES 32

Are you going for

dinner out? "Moderation too
much"—you clucking. Well:
fancy it crave don't

feed no wiser a
stomach or push living
a spell endure sick.
There's yesterday a doctor.
About the nutrition is

everything you gotta eat
natural. So where find
always anywhere this natural?
Would fib lots stores
from label truth. Is
bodies differing machines built
to same behave?

YINGLISH STROPHES 33

Poetry is just for

sense yourself feelings from
pondering in. To make
a living doesn't flow

that river. You took
up a profession that
kills the eyes. What
painters I'll museum for?
The clear good ones

I can stay from far
shadows bloom sunning bright with
people crowd or few, only.
Rembrandt—he's my pet painter.
We saw all his life.
Was going in a series.
Picasso—he's new to me.

YINGLISH STROPHES 34

Noise up culture countering. Those

hippies! Still coverage they count
extreme the media. Why not
of your origin be civil?

Who else could blanketing you
that much? Your father— not
so natured ill. Only want
for him each items nice folded.
Mine: from me early cut ambulance

succumbs the house. To grow of
understanding you'll older sweeten, Too hippies
maybe. I have for you chocolate

cake a piece. Come. I have.

YINGLISH STROPHES 35

They board, lonely, gregarious,

a warp time. Stereotypists
through decade fifties presuming
universe placid then—when

regions not kissed of
media screaming actual. And
those twenties wouldn't see
some dinge alleys roaring.
To whimper, poverished. Well,

rain of error can
refreshes daily today
an instant small. So
practical everyone could admire
big monument (fried verily
rubric) until to near
enough smelling sick breath.

YNGLISH STROPHES 36

Madcap baseball banshee: "brotherhood"

in proliferate to xenophobes.
Wouldn't my door knock
cheerful. Would apart knock

down. Their forebears from
far. As me. Across.
Not here Indians as
always. Precious to this
land you boat or

plane reaching, deep night
scurries border through—no
facts announces none couldn't
contribute e pluribus as
unum much. Finding also
born citizens produce lazy,
making ineptitude, honest not.

THE EXTRAS

blindly,   often
obsequiously solicited praise.
At last—   former extras.
Adulation
roosts
on them.   A human

kiss.

Not long until   monotone
plethora, fanatic condescension
idolatry, ruptured relaxation
lead to   fabrication
of   glazed boozers
& boor glaciers.

IN A LUMINOUS

dark, bleachers
bleach. A beard is
no protection against a lit match, grift(ing) preachers.
Hey, don't hog those
fried slogans!
Muffled soloist's heart has eyes

for stone rose. As

if a knockout proves
virtue. Inveterate theme jumper forfeits
message consistency for road marriages
in a velvet truck. Dwindles
before our ears.
Concentration of sorrow in the punchbowl.

TRANSITIONAL OBJECTS

Silt-blazed goggles,
nylon

stalagmites, gargoyle
replica threaded by weevil
garland.

Compact rainbow citadel?
Parents, offspring move away.
Many an item stays.
Planning to mount that dandelion

Stepladder? (Beside understated harpoon.)
Long untuned cello
grunts: "Aren't all
grand
transitions firmly in the past?

Save the last."

CAGE SINGS

Alley cats
comb through

catacombs. Neighbors
wade in
our trash.

The Academy
is snatching

back your Oscar.

GOAD 27

—for J.S. Strifling

Glittering smoke rises from reality roses. Even a bestselling
agent can't move a dingy cellar. Presumption of innocence is
strained: don't you
recognize the baggage
on that carousel?
One can't imagine a
permit granted for
that murder weapon. Due
process aside, the defense
writhes. Sensing what it has
accomplished, the rifle weeps.

GOAD 28

The kids don't wear watches no more. Those phone-
computers wipe their asses and everything. Drenched in pharma
ceutical opera, they
drag race on imaginary
highways & skid into
the palace of error. (No,
it's not my cane & white
locks talkin'.) Reason may
adopt a rhythm, but rhythm
ain't reason. Will the kids ever
locate invisible light?

GOAD 29

“The world has flattened,” whines the surfer who
suffers undersized waves. Nagging a tide into compliance
materializes only in ahistori
cal fictions. Not that
he’s con sidered
packing up gear
& waiting a spell or
motoring to another
beach. One should
try out nearly any strata
gem but tedious despair.

GOAD 30

<pre>
   Do I ever catch   myself vamping like a rhetorical vulture
as I   pounce   on parodies of love & gooey remnants of
                 boiled   vignettes from
              friendships   that passed out—
           deceptions   ago? Sustained,
          but not sustain   able. Imagin
           ation deferred.   Delinquent
              sonata fodder   smeared on
                     a bulb   or   two?
</pre>

GOAD 31

Could parental indifference & idolatry spawn the same
imbalance? Our "conversation" got stuck on your alleged
perfections & coruscating
triumphs. Furor at
invisible snarls, in
audible snipes
placed second.
None of this has
been re corded.
Curiosity about
other minds: credit or
debit? Assert ion chases
"objective" value. Is the cor
oner around the corner?

GOAD 32

How many homes do they own this week?
Where do they drop their sleek, plump, fresh-
smelling leftovers? What
radical narcissism
can muster:
"I appreciate
your appreciation.
By exten sion, you."
Resplendent commodity ex
istence: precipice of joy.

ANONYMOUS APOSTROPHE

Skies
drain. Baritone birds
plug a gap in melody. Theirs
is
inhuman. One high-pitched side
of a call stretches
from Cold Spring
Harbor to
Jamaica. A stranger
could profit
from that
kibitzing about
loose screws
in the superstructure—
& how to
tighten
them.

PROXIMITY

If I put on
my glasses, I'll be able to hear
you. Desert
river?
Bleached symphony? Tarnished

soap fat melting. Cloudsword
slicing a grand
mountain
midsection?

"You are
too close to the art.
Please step away." No parking

in the tender
zone?

TERSE RHYMES 1

Shell

frame:

harass

restrain.

Glass.

Shame

name.

Maim.

Hell.

TERSE RHYMES 2

Aperture

allure.

Face

obscure.

Chase

ace.

Brace

for

war.

TERSE RHYMES 3

Pew

Smell

insist

sin-

kissed

tryst

fall

to

install

guilt

sprawl.

Silt,
rust,
dust.
Hell
fist.
Trust
In
small
mist
wall?

TERSE RHYMES 4

Tend

friend.

Heed

bleed.
Upend

weed.

Plead,

mend.

Lead,

bend.

Read

trend.

Breed

blend.
Feed.
End
need.

TERSE RHYMES 5

Dither

Rainbow

snow

or

taper

star

vapor.

Basis

collar?

Below

stasis:

wither.

TERSE RHYMES 6

Crumb—
bait
serve
hum
urge:
raw
feast
surge.
Inviting
splurge.
Defense

swerve:

unnerve,

berate,

indicting

claw.

Inciting

intense

"beast"

purge.

TERSE RHYMES 7

Behind
brine
grind,
din,
bind,
thin
through
spine,
avenue
spin
to
mine
new
sign.
You
begin
to
realign
mind
skin,
to
redesign
vine
sinew,

accrue

refined

line.

TERSE RHYMES 8

Core

vexation

bray.

How

stupid

determinism

can

fix
&
fan
attraction,
brand
one-
way
fixation.
Nix
or

endow

Cupid
v traction,

plant

instant

schism.

TERSE RHYMES 9

Snow

sting.

Narrow

rote

doubt—

snake

anew.

Devout

coat

cling.

You

burrow

below

ache

to

remote

wing.

TERSE RHYMES 10

Bypass
latest
bombast
blast.

Protest

crass

heap

creep.

Bleep

chagrin

morass.

Invest

fast

in

fittest

deep

nest;
reap
honest
sleep.

TERSE RHYMES 11

(One may)

flutter,
shudder,

stutter,
blubber,
sputter,

mutter

(yet still)

utter.

RAIN

embroidery.

Chiaroscuro
bloodstream.

Immaterial sky
without horizon
marks.

DUSK BOWL INTIMACIES 38

So the gorgeous trendsetters are short on magnificent monograms?
Please don't pester me with cuddly word pictures tumbling out of
a small device, my pale pal. Sinuous insinuations for stay-at-home
brains. Like Botox for a sticky persona. Novelty is beyond our reach.
I'm hankering instead for a visionary insurance agent, blonde as night.

Providing
umbrella coverage
against all horror.

DUSK BOWL INTIMACIES 39

I woke up with a different mouth. Where would I have misplaced the old version? Compulsive lawyers rush to take my pulse. They advocate a new spiffy suit. At best a glowing (glowering?) diversion, as heredity creaks on. Earlier environmental touchstones have not.

Ratty
plastic sleeves
constrict shriveled photos.

SOME EYES

supply
a false positive, though less
frequently
than smiles.
As
master
listeners
intuit, any
voice reveals.
When I sat alone today
with my
liver
sandwich, it loved me unconditionally
up to the final bite. Do not judge my
likely
value to your
rising action until the lamp is
spent, & you can only
hear.

BONE TELEVISION

Botched orchard.
Evaporating ground.
Branches shrinking.
Night writing

bone

television.

Stump accumulates
moonlight. Vertebrae
exhale inside
glass page.

JIGSAW HUBBUB 24

Eavesdrop soup—gallons of
it—could make that
one lone bystander
subservient to melancholic
churn. Magnets & magnates
are loosely clust ered tonight.
They splurge on spitfire person
ality, flashing blind allegiance
to devastating wardrobes. As
most plug into drifts of presumed
gratification, would their
bubbles ever reveal contented
thoughts— much less
joy? The sideliner
lacks the digestive
system for blazing
party immersion. She'd welcome
untrammeled one on one recognition.

JIGSAW HUBBUB 25

Sporadically, tactical alliances—
founded on impact
smiles, esteemed
plastics, & the promise
of revolut ionary
desserts— flash imi
tations of morale.
However, a norm of
traded tirades & foible
generators is turning this
body into an irrelevant sub
committee of a subcommittee,
where familiar bullshit gets sold
by volume, not by weight. My hair
hears myriad equities retreating.
In one's mental backyard, is the
ghoul of fatal spending ever
absent? Most members who
've endured a career yo-yo will
cling to this chronic futility. But your
contacts beyond the conference
room whisper of a cogent lever cluster,
well sequestered from official machinery.
Why not do your damnedest to listen?

JIGSAW HUBBUB 26

One hope: that the list of
spirits in a high-end
jukebox heralds
a lasting bonanza
license. Today, you select
crooner radia tion. The one
with the golden button.
From a dream cabinet
wafts piano sirloin. Separate,
inseparable from adjacent
midriffs commencing
to riff. Mur murs inexhaust
ible? Sure, let's get attuned to
yet not enveloped by stammering
holograms. Some darker violin
inquiry should not atrophy.

REVERSE MONOBON: REVIEW OF YESTERHOUR'S COMPUTER DIET

—for Mark Young

Tell me how an octopus is contained in an octagon.

Must communist pentameter succumb to imperial ethos? Are these tightrope drunkards or silk critics sparring in a rumor-padded e-seminar cell over cancel couture? Can a populist viscountess in amethyst spangles settle the dustup? Does it empower us to embrace previously hidden links among the social tropologies of bracelet, brace, and bracket? For those at loggerheads over causes and consequences of alien oil dependency and its intersection with thermostat panic, videos of last September's flowering embers may not quite douse those flames. Rather than clicking on professional indiscretion-prodigies secreting spasmodic, boast-riddled oratorios or ice cream impressions purported to zap "anyone" out of anhedonia, I sped to the amendment of a guidebook entry on a palace now known to be funded by kleptomaniacs. Take heart, though: there's no shortage of sledgehammer visionaries bent on recycling degenerate sepulchers into sustainable barns.

Note: Eileen R. Tabios recently invented the monobon, a prose poem followed by a monostich.

HARD COPY

is no

longer accepted.

Too visceral.

A forceful

void reaches

far into

the impressionable….

THREATLESS

Ready

to ditch language fetters, dump moldy
software? To get
active accessing survival

vocabulary?
Those who call it
"cramming your skull
with extraneous data" are musty
oppressors. No end user need slide into affective frugality

or curb reasonable
soul
sprawl.
Bonus: innovative password crafting for your 78 accounts will
retard cognitive decline until
parts have worn out.
If you decline to submit

to the new technology,
it
will
destabilize your epistemological
welfare & your ontological
security.
Not
a threat.
Mere fact.

DISCERNMENT

Where screams are
routine, overflowing
tubs of data.
Much pickled
in inference bilge.
If dice

could riot.... Militant

entertainers claiming
force to
encapsulate truth
trends. An earnest
listening face.
Drowsy ears.

TROJAN PANOPTICON 6

From rumpled skeletons, spiritual
termites sashay
into a center.
Unbleached odor
delivers bouncy indifference to

punchbowl civility. Gentle
bomb dustbin
cloudburst, toupees
boogying. Web
stampede? Sparkling cess

pool. Bombards with sedatives.
Best to flush that
rancid sunset.
Inaudible strings
subtend abyss stunts. No owl

fur frock today: your prime
fashion cynosure
catwalks those rags
that first knew her.
Nearly 10 welts ago. Blessed

with pseudonymous pro
tection, we are
shirking technical
quandary duty
until noticed further.

TROJAN PANOPTICON 7

Musk & muck of online play
ground. Eroding
firmament communion.
Slurping off soggy
myth plates. Bedeviled cathedral

hustlers miking invisible eruption
purrs, alleging
infernos, concocting
ecstasies. To reap
wall control, backchanneled lucre.

TROJAN PANOPTICON 8

Inside wallpaper, inhuman educators
steer miscellany
cruise. Will you
disembark at Mis
anthrope Alley, where silk critics lob

long- rage missiles at sleepwalkers'
daydream dregs or at
Luxury Tasteland,
where an isometric
jukebox's sandblasting contemporary

lyre solicits cosmopolitan workout
drool & galvanizes
amoeba vantage-
perches & galactic playrooms?

TROJAN PANOPTICON 9

Fecklessly accumulating catalog
of cata strophes.
Blunder gobs. Cavern
or tavern matrix weavers
facilitate plonk conclaves airing

psychotic maximum to squirt
out old hates.
Illiterate litanies
miked to blare on.
Cobwebs impervious to a pot

ent spray. Yet fertile daydream
ing will not de
siccate or resign itself
to insub stantiality.
Are ocean's octaves audible?

ARTIFICIAL STUPEFACTION

When a system's

unleashed to spew
nearly infinite inhuman behaviors,

fruits
may be intended for immature audiences.
Syntax

janitors
are banging heads
against a cloud barricade. Will schools
float in psychotic soufflé?

Acknowledgments

Grateful acknowledgment is made to publications where poems appeared, sometimes in different versions:

BlazeVox: "A Brief Survey"; "Anonymous Apostrophe"; "CEO Collides with Brute Paradox"; "Cold Calling"; "Hidden in Plain Site"

Halo Halo Review: "Reverse Monobon: Review of Yesterhour's Computer Diet"

Marsh Hawk Review: "In a Luminous"; "The Café Drugs"

Moss Trill: "Terse Rhymes 8"

Otoliths: "Terse Rhymes 1-4"; "Sartorial Ideologies '68"; "Trend Spin"

Posit: "Yinglish Strophes 31-34"

Survision: "Bone Television"; "'You Get What You Pay For'"

Synchronized Chaos: "Goad 27-28"; "Memory Tactics"

TXTOBJX: "Terse Rhymes 5"

Unlikely Stories Mark V: "Affront to Center and Circumference," "Bureau," and "Galvanizing Jumble"

Utriculi: "Loss," "Remain Seated," "Some Eyes," "The Extras"

I would like to thank Eileen R. Tabios for her superb editorial suggestions.

About the Author

Thomas Fink has published 12 previous books of poetry—most recently *Zeugma* (Marsh Hawk Press, 2022) and *A Pageant for Every Addiction* (Marsh Hawk, 2020), written collaboratively with Maya D. Mason. His *Selected Poems & Poetic Series* appeared in 2016. He is the author of *Reading Poetry with College and University Students: Overcoming Barriers and Deepening Engagement* (Bloomsbury Academic, 2022), as well as two books of criticism, and three edited anthologies. His work appeared in *Best American Poetry 2007*. Fink's paintings hang in various collections. He is Professor of English at CUNY-LaGuardia.

Titles From Marsh Hawk Press

Jane Augustine *Arbor Vitae; Krazy; Night Lights; A Woman's Guide to Mountain Climbing*
Tom Beckett *~~Dipstick~~ (Diptych)*
William Benton *Light on Water*
Sigman Byrd *Under the Wanderer's Star*
Patricia Carlin: *Original Green; Quantum Jitters; Second Nature*
Claudia Carlson *The Elephant House; My Chocolate Sarcophagus; Pocket Park*
Lorna Dee Cervantes: *April on Olympia*
Meredith Cole *Miniatures*
Jon Curley *The Installation of Fear; Hybrid Moments; Scorch Marks; Remnant Halo*
Joanne D. Dwyer *RASA*
Neil de la Flor *Almost Dorothy; An Elephant's Memory of Blizzards*
Chard deNiord *Sharp Golden Thorn*
Sharon Dolin *Serious Pink*
Joanne Dominique Dwyer *Rasa*
Steve Fellner *Blind Date with Cavafy; The Weary World Rejoices*
Thomas Fink *Zeugma, Selected Poems & Poetic Series; Joyride; Peace Conference; Clarity and Other Poems; After Taxes; Gossip*
Thomas Fink and Maya D. Mason *A Pageant for Every Addiction*
Norman Finkelstein *Inside the Ghost Factory; Passing Over*
Edward Foster *A Looking-Glass for Traytors; The Beginning of Sorrows; Dire Straits; Mahrem: Things Men Should Do for Men; Sewing the Wind; What He Ought to Know*
Paolo Javier *The Feeling is Actual*
Burt Kimmelman *Abandoned Angel; Somehow; Steeple at Sunrise; Zero Point Poiesis;* with Fred Caruso *The Pond at Cape May Point*
Basil King *Disparate Beasts: Part Two; 77 Beasts; Disparate Beasts; Mirage; The Spoken Word / The Painted Hand from Learning to Draw / A History*
Martha King *Imperfect Fit*
David Lehman *The Birth of* The Best
Phillip Lopate *At the End of the Day*
Mary Mackey *Breaking the Fever; The Jaguars That Prowl Our Dreams; Sugar Zone; Travelers With No Ticket Home; Creativity*
Jason McCall *Dear Hero*
Sandy McIntosh *The After-Death History of My Mother; Between Earth and Sky; Cemetery Chess; Ernesta, in the Style of the Flamenco; Forty-Nine Guaranteed Ways to Escape Death; A Hole In the Ocean; Lesser Lights; Obsessional; Plan B:*
Stephen Paul Miller *Any Lie You Tell Will Be the Truth; The Bee Flies in May; Fort Dad; Skinny Eighth Avenue; There's Only One God and You're Not It*
Daniel Morris *Blue Poles; Bryce Passage; Hit Play; If Not for the Courage*
Gail Newman *Blood Memory*
Geoffrey O'Brien *Where Did Poetry Come From; The Blue Hill*
Sharon Olinka *The Good City*
Christina Olivares *No Map of the Earth Includes Stars*
Justin Petropoulos *Eminent Domain*
Paul Pines *Charlotte Songs; Divine Madness; Gathering Sparks; Last Call at the Tin Palace*
Jacquelyn Pope *Watermark*
George Quasha *Things Done for Themselves*
Karin Randolph *Either She Was*
Rochelle Ratner *Balancing Acts; Ben Casey Days; House and Home*
Michael Rerick *In Ways Impossible to Fold*
Corrine Robins *Facing It; One Thousand Years; Today's Menu*
Liane Strauss *The Flaws in the Story*
Eileen R. Tabios *The Inventor: A Poet's Transcolonial Autobiography; Because I Love You I Become War; The Connoisseur of Alleys; I Take Thee, English, for My Beloved; The In(ter)vention of the Hay(na)ku; The Light Sang as It Left Your Eyes; Reproductions of the Empty Flagpole; Sun Stigmata; The Thorn Rosary* with j/j hastain *The Relational Elations of Orphaned Algebra*
Tony Trigilio: *Proof Something Happened; Craft: A Memoir*
Susan Terris *Green Leaves Unseeing; Familiar Tense; Ghost of Yesterday; Natural Defenses*
Lynne Thompson *Fretwork*
Madeline Tiger *Birds of Sorrow and Joy*
Tana Jean Welch *Latest Volcano*
Harriet Zinnes: D*rawing on the Wall; Light Light or the Curvature of the Earth; New and Selected Poems; Weather is Whether; Whither Nonstopping*
Xiaoqiu Qiu: *Other Side of Ocean* (anthology) *On Becoming a Poet*

YEAR	AUTHOR	TITLE	JUDGE
2004	Jacquelyn Pope	*Watermark*	Marie Ponsot
2005	Sigman Byrd	*Under the Wanderer's Star*	Gerald Stern
2006	Steve Fellner	*Blind Date with Cavafy*	Denise Duhamel
2007	Karin Randolph	*Either She Was*	David Shapiro
2008	Michael Rerick	*In Ways Impossible to Fold*	Thylias Moss
2009	Neil de la Flor	*Almost Dorothy*	Forrest Gander
2010	Justin Petropoulos	*Eminent Domain*	Anne Waldman
2011	Meredith Cole	*Miniatures*	Alicia Ostriker
2012	Jason McCall	*Dear Hero,*	Cornelius Eady
2013	Tom Beckett	*~~Dipstick~~ (Diptych)*	Charles Bernstein
2014	Christina Olivares	*No Map of the Earth Includes Stars*	Brenda Hillman
2015	Tana Jean Welch	*Latest Volcano*	Stephanie Strickland
2016	Robert Gibb	*After*	Mark Doty
2017	Geoffrey O'Brien	*The Blue Hill*	Meena Alexander
2018	Lynne Thompson	*Fretwork*	Jane Hirshfield
2019	Gail Newman	*Blood Memory*	Marge Piercy
2020	Tony Trigilio	*Proof Something Happened*	Susan Howe
2021	Joanne D. Dwyer	*Rasa*	David Lehman
2022	Brian Cochran	*Translation Zone*	John Yau
2023	Liane Strauss	*The Flaws in the Story*	Mary Jo Bang
2024	Xiaoqiu Qiu	*Other Side of Ocean*	John Keene